Vampire Bats

by Anne Welsbacher

Consultant:
Kimberly Joan Williams
Executive Director
Organization for Bat Conservation

CAPSTONE
HIGH-INTEREST
BOOKS

Capstone High-Interest Books are published by Capstone Press
151 Good Counsel Drive, P.O. Box 669, Mankato, Minnesota 56002
http://www.capstone-press.com

Library of Congress Cataloging-in-Publication Data
Welsbacher, Anne, 1955-
   Vampire bats/by Anne Welsbacher.
   p. cm.—(Predators in the wild)
   Includes bibliographical references (p. 31) and index.
   ISBN 0-7368-0787-X
   1. Desmodus rotundus—Juvenile literature. [1. Vampire bats.
2. Bats.] I. Title. II. Series.
QL737.C52 W45 2001
599.4'5—dc21   00-009988

Summary: Describes vampire bats, their habits, where they live, their hunting
methods, and how they exist in the world of people.

Editorial Credits
Blake Hoena, editor; Karen Risch, product planning editor; Timothy Halldin,
   cover designer and illustrator; Katy Kudela, photo researcher

Photo Credits
Gary Milburn/TOM STACK & ASSOCIATES, 12, 14
Kim Williams/Organization for Bat Conservation, 10, 16
Michael Cardwell/Extreme Wildlife Photography, cover
M. P. L. Fogden/Bruce Coleman Inc., 18
Rob and Ann Simpson, 29
Robert & Linda Mitchell, 6, 8, 21, 22
Roger Rageot/David Liebman, 9, 11 (top), 11 (bottom), 15, 20, 24, 27

1 2 3 4 5 6 06 05 04 03 02 01

Table of Contents

Common name: Vampire bat

Scientific names: *Desmodus rotundus* (common vampire bat)

Diaemus youngi (white-winged vampire bat)

Diphylla ecaudata (hairy-legged vampire bat)

Average size: Vampire bats grow 2.75 to 3.5 inches (7 to 9 centimeters) long.

Average weight: Vampire bats weigh between 1 and 1.75 ounces (30 and 50 grams).

Wingspan: Vampire bats' wingspans are between 13 and 15 inches (33 and 38 centimeters) wide.

Life span: Vampire bats live 9 to 20 years.

Skills: Vampire bats are able to walk on the ground. They also hop, leap, and perform somersaults.

Habitat: Vampire bats may live in hollow trees, empty buildings, mines, and wells. Vampire bat colonies usually include 20 to 100 bats. Some colonies can have as many as 5,000 bats.

Prey: Vampire bats drink the blood of other animals. These animals may include cows, horses, mules, birds, and pigs.

Social habits: Vampire bats share food with hungry members of their roost. Female vampire bats often form long-term relationships with other females.

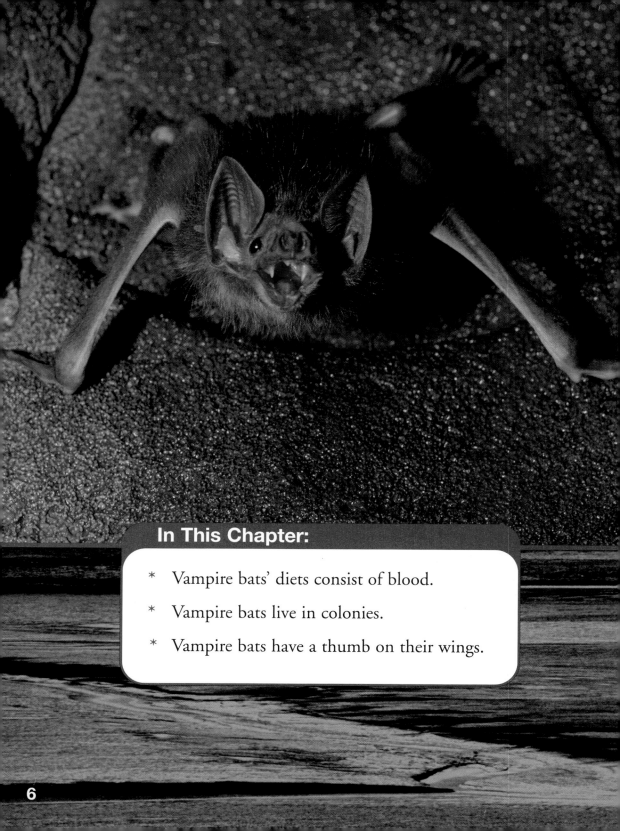

In This Chapter:

* Vampire bats' diets consist of blood.

* Vampire bats live in colonies.

* Vampire bats have a thumb on their wings.

Chapter 1

Vampire Bats

Vampire bats have an unusual diet. They eat blood. They are the only mammal with this strange diet.

Bat Species

Almost 1,000 bat species exist in the world. Species are specific types of animals.

There are three species of vampire bats. *Desmodus rotundus* is the scientific name for the common vampire bat. *Diaemus youngi* is the scientific name for the white-winged vampire bat. *Diphylla ecaudata* is the third vampire bat species. This bat species also is called the hairy-legged vampire bat.

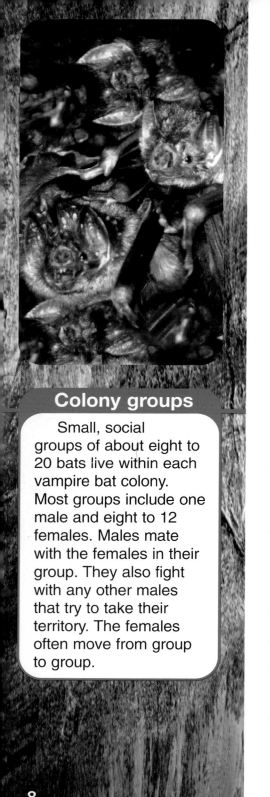

Colony groups

Small, social groups of about eight to 20 bats live within each vampire bat colony. Most groups include one male and eight to 12 females. Males mate with the females in their group. They also fight with any other males that try to take their territory. The females often move from group to group.

Where They Live

Vampire bats are sensitive to cold and hot weather. They cannot live in places that are too cold or too hot. Vampire bats live in Mexico, Central America, and South America.

Vampire bats live in colonies. These groups usually include 20 to 100 bats. But colonies may have as many as 5,000 bats.

Vampire bat colonies live in caves, hollow trees, empty buildings, mines, and wells. These places are dark and cool.

Appearance

Vampire bats have red, gold, or gray-brown fur. The fur is darker on their backs than it is on their stomachs. This coloring helps to camouflage them. From above, the dark fur on their backs looks like

Vampire bats may live in caves.

the ground. From below, the light fur on their stomachs looks like the sky.

Vampire bats are small. They can fit into a person's palm. They grow 2.75 to 3.5 inches (7 to 9 centimeters) long. They weigh only 1 to 1.75 ounces (30 to 50 grams).

Vampire bats are good climbers.

Special Abilities

Vampire bats are strong for their size. They can use their front legs and chest muscles for many purposes. They can run, climb walls, hop, and leap into the air. They can even perform somersaults. These movements help vampire bats sneak up on prey. They also help vampire bats avoid being injured by prey's movements.

Vampire bats have a special thumb on their wings. This thumb is .6 to .75 inches (1.5 to 1.9 centimeters) long. It helps vampire bats balance on the ground when they walk. It also helps them push off the ground as they jump into the air.

Flying

Vampire bats' wingspans are 13 to 15 inches (33 to 38 centimeters) wide. Vampire bats' wings are covered with a very thin membrane. This skin is so thin that light can pass through it.

Vampire bats can fold their wings close to their bodies. This action allows them to squeeze into small places.

Vampire bats fly well. They fly closer to the ground than other bats do. Most bats fly high in the air to catch insects. Vampire bats fly close to the ground to sneak up on their prey. Vampire bats can fly six to 12 miles (9.7 to 19 kilometers) per hour. But they cannot fly long distances.

Vampire bats sometimes are so full after feeding that they cannot fly. They then may rest in a nearby tree before flying back to their roost.

Wingspan

Thumb

In This Chapter:

* Vampire bats sneak up on their prey.

* Vampire bats use echolocation.

* Vampire bats are nocturnal.

Chapter 2

The Hunt

Vampire bats drink the blood of cows and horses. They sometimes feed on pigs, dogs, birds, and people. Vampire bats sneak up on their prey. They often do this while their prey sleeps.

Vampire bats' strong sense of smell allows them to locate prey. It also allows them to locate certain animals. For example, vampire bats can tell one cow from another in a large herd. This ability helps them locate prey that they have bitten before. Vampire bats often feed on the same animal night after night.

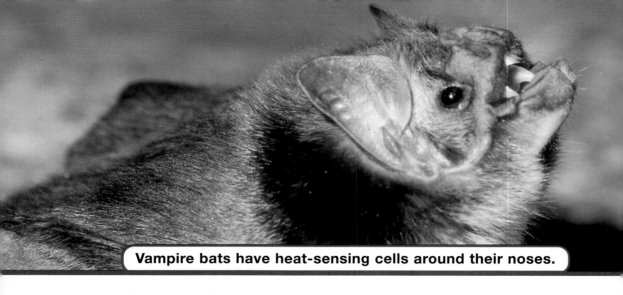

Vampire bats have heat-sensing cells around their noses.

Special Senses

Like many bats, vampire bats use echolocation. They make a high-pitched sound with their mouth and nose. This sound then bounces off objects. The sound's echo helps bats detect objects as they fly. Most bats use echolocation to find prey. But vampire bats mainly use it to find their way at night. Echolocation helps vampire bats avoid objects while flying.

Vampire bats have heat-sensing cells around their noses. They use these cells to locate warm areas on their prey's skin. In warm areas, blood vessels are near the skin's surface. These narrow tubes carry blood throughout animals' bodies. Vampire bats feed on the blood in blood vessels.

Vampire bats feed on blood vessels near the skin's surface.

Vampire bats sneak up on their prey.

Seeking Prey

Vampire bats are nocturnal. They hunt at night. During a full moon, they sometimes wait until the moon has set before hunting. Darkness allows vampire bats to sneak up on their prey. It also protects them from predators.

Owls, snakes, and hawks may prey on vampire bats.

Vampire bats seek prey that they can sneak up on. They choose animals near the edge of a herd. They prefer animals that are in woods rather than animals in open fields. Vampire bats also usually feed on sleeping animals.

Vampire bats fly around 6 to 8 feet (1.8 to 2.4 meters) above the ground when seeking prey. They then may land on their prey. Most prey animals do not notice vampire bats because of their small size.

Vampire bats also may land on the ground near their prey. They then walk up to their prey. Vampire bats either climb or jump onto their prey. Their slow, careful movements often prevent them from being noticed by other animals.

Vampire bats then seek out a spot to bite their prey. They choose a spot where blood vessels are close to the skin. Vampire bats may bite their prey on the shoulder or neck. They often bite cows just above their hooves. They may bite pigs and dogs on their noses. Blood vessels are close to the skin in these areas.

In This Chapter:

* Vampire bats have sharp, pointed incisors.

* Vampire bats share food.

* Coagulants cause blood to clot.

Chapter 3

Drawing Blood

Vampire bats do not seriously hurt their prey when they feed. They do not drink enough blood to harm animals. But animals sometimes feel the vampire bats. These animals then may try to remove the vampire bats. They do this by shaking, swatting their tail, or brushing up against a tree. If this happens, vampire bats jump off their prey and wait nearby. When their prey settles down, they try to feed again.

Vampire bats often return to bite the same animal night after night. They re-open the wound that they made before. This action is easier than making a new wound on a different animal.

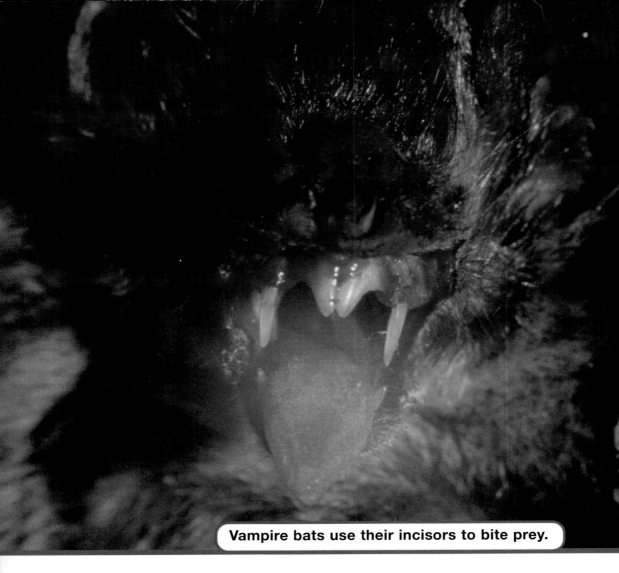

Vampire bats use their incisors to bite prey.

The Bite

Vampire bats use their upper incisors to bite their prey. These front teeth are sharp and pointed. A vampire bat's bite creates a wound less than .2 inches (5 millimeters) deep. Most animals do not notice a vampire bat's bite.

As they bite, vampire bats grab their prey's skin with their lower incisors. They then slide their tongue between these teeth to lick the wound. Their tongue fits into a groove in their lower lip.

Vampire bats have two channels on the bottom of their tongue. These openings work like straws. Vampire bats suck blood through them. At the same time, they flick blood into their mouth with their tongue. Vampire bats can flick their tongue four times per second. This action makes their head nod back and forth while they feed.

Vampire bats urinate while they feed. This action removes extra fluids from their bodies. They then can drink more blood. Vampire bats feed for 10 to 30 minutes.

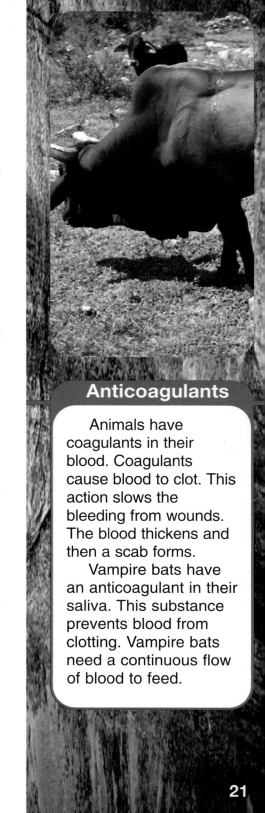

Anticoagulants

Animals have coagulants in their blood. Coagulants cause blood to clot. This action slows the bleeding from wounds. The blood thickens and then a scab forms.

Vampire bats have an anticoagulant in their saliva. This substance prevents blood from clotting. Vampire bats need a continuous flow of blood to feed.

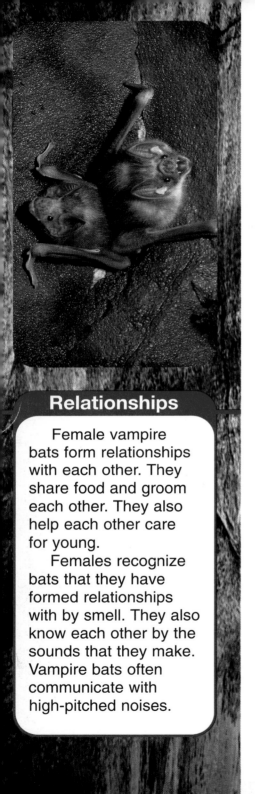

Relationships

Female vampire bats form relationships with each other. They share food and groom each other. They also help each other care for young.

Females recognize bats that they have formed relationships with by smell. They also know each other by the sounds that they make. Vampire bats often communicate with high-pitched noises.

Sharing Food

Vampire bats sometimes share food with other bats in their roost. Hyenas, wild dogs, chimpanzees, and people are other animals that share food.

Vampire bats cannot live more than two or three nights without feeding. Each night, one or two out of every six bats will not find food. Bats that successfully feed often share food with hungry bats. They do this by regurgitating their food. Vampire bats vomit blood into hungry bats' mouths.

Most often, females share food with each other. A hungry female will groom another female for several minutes. The second female will then regurgitate food into the hungry female's mouth.

Myth: Vampire bats are dangerous to people.

Fact: Vampire bats are shy and hide from people. They do not bite deeply enough to seriously injure prey. Vampire bats do bite people. But they prefer cattle, horses, or pigs.

Myth: Vampire bats can smell blood.

Fact: Vampire bats have a strong sense of smell. But they smell their prey and not blood.

Myth: Vampire bats are blind.

Fact: All bats are able to see.

Myth: Vampire bats are dirty.

Fact: Vampire bats are very clean. They often groom themselves and their roost mates.

In This Chapter:

* Vampire bats can spread diseases.

* People try to control vampire bat populations.

* Vampire bats benefit people and other animals.

Chapter 4

In the World of People

Today, more vampire bats live in areas where people live. People cut down forests in South and Central America to make ranches and farms. They keep large herds of cattle in these areas. These herds attract vampire bats. Vampire bats easily can find these groups of animals to feed on. It is much more difficult for vampire bats to find wild prey.

People in these areas sometimes wake to find blood on their sheets and bed. They felt no pain as they slept. But they have been bitten by a vampire bat. Once bitten, that person is more likely to be bitten again. Vampire bats like to feed off existing wounds.

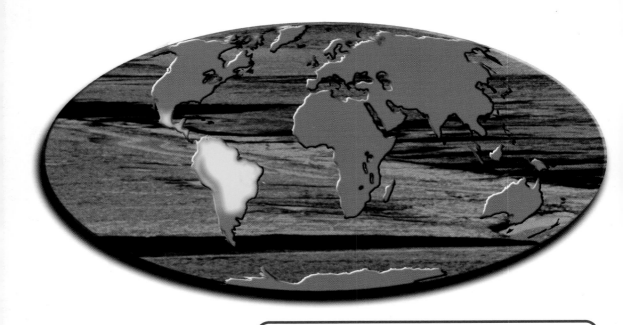

Yellow represents the vampire bat's range.

Diseases

Vampire bats do not drink enough blood to harm their prey. But their bites can become infected by germs. Diseases and infections are the greatest danger from vampire bat bites.

Rabies is spread by bites from infected animals. This disease is deadly if not treated. In the 1920s, scientists learned that infected vampire bats can spread rabies.

Battling Vampire Bats

In the mid-1900s, people began to fight vampire bats in two ways. First, they protected themselves and their animals. They used fences and bright lights to try to keep vampire bats away. They made new vaccines. These medicines protected animals from diseases spread by vampire bat bites.

People also killed vampire bats. They used dynamite to blow up caves where the bats lived. They also used poisonous gases to kill vampire bats.

In 1967, scientists began to research ways to control vampire bats. These scientists discovered that anticoagulant drugs caused bleeding in vampire bats. These drugs keep blood from clotting. The bats given these drugs bleed to death.

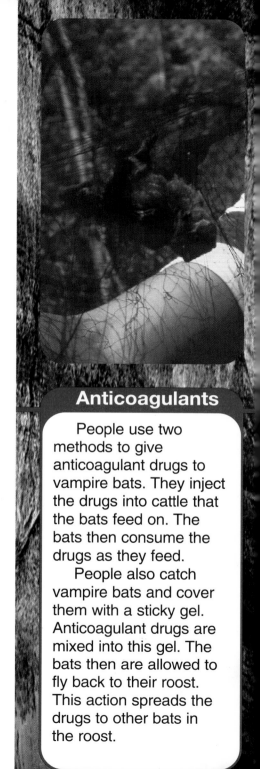

Anticoagulants

People use two methods to give anticoagulant drugs to vampire bats. They inject the drugs into cattle that the bats feed on. The bats then consume the drugs as they feed.

People also catch vampire bats and cover them with a sticky gel. Anticoagulant drugs are mixed into this gel. The bats then are allowed to fly back to their roost. This action spreads the drugs to other bats in the roost.

Vampire Bat Benefits

Vampire bats can benefit other animals. A vampire bat may feed on several animals in a night. This action can spread antibodies for a disease from one animal to another. Antibodies in animals' blood help them fight infections and diseases.

Vampire bats also help people. The anticoagulant in vampires bats' saliva works better than human-made anticoagulants. Scientists have developed the drug Diaculin from vampire bat anticoagulant. This drug is used to help people with heart diseases. Diaculin thins blood. This action helps the heart pump blood through the body.

Rugged Survivors

People often fear and misunderstand bats. Today, many of the bats in North and South America are on the endangered species list. Animals on this list are in danger of dying out.

The common vampire bat is not currently on this list. Large populations of vampire bats

Vampire bats are not on the endangered species list.

exist in South and Central America. But scientists do not know how many white-winged and hairy-legged vampire bats exist. They believe that these bats are more rare than the common vampire bat.

anticoagulant (an-ti-koh-AG-yuh-lant)—a substance that stops blood from clotting

camouflage (KAM-uh-flahzh)—coloring or covering that makes animals, people, and objects look like their surroundings

echolocation (ek-oh-loh-KAY-shuhn)—the process of using sounds and echoes to locate objects; vampire bats use echolocation to locate objects while flying at night.

incisor (in-SY-zor)—a sharp, pointed tooth

membrane (MEM-brayn)—a thin layer of skin

nocturnal (nok-TUR-nuhl)—active at night

regurgitate (ree-GUR-juh-tate)—to vomit food after it has been eaten

vaccine (vak-SEEN)—medicine that protects against diseases

To Learn More

Blair, Diane and Pamela Wright. *Bat Watching*. Wildlife Watching. Mankato, Minn.: Capstone High-Interest Books, 2000.

Gerholdt, Pamela J. *Vampire Bats*. Checkerboard Animal Library. Edina, Minn.: Abdo & Daughters, 1996.

Greenaway, Theresa. *The Really Fearsome Blood-Loving Vampire Bat: and Other Creatures with Strange Eating Habits*. The Really Horrible Guides. New York: DK Publishing, 1996

Useful Addresses

Bat Conservation International
P.O. Box 162603
Austin, TX 78716

The Organization for Bat Conservation
1553 Haslett Road
Haslett, MI 48840

Bat Conservation Society of Canada
P.O. Box 56042
Calgary, AB T2E 8K5
Canada

Internet Sites

Bats Bats Everywhere
http://members.aol.com/bats4kids

Bat Conservation International
http://www.batcon.org

Canadian Bat Resources
http://www.cancaver.ca/bats

Organization for Bat Conservation
http://www.batconservation.org

Index